Connellsville, Pa.

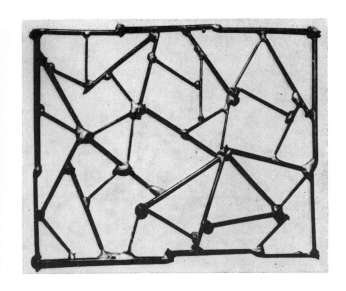

elmar gruber

NAIL SCULPTURE

**LITTLE
CRAFT BOOK
SERIES**

STERLING PUBLISHING CO., INC.   NEW YORK

The Oak Tree Press   LONDON AND SYDNEY

Little Craft Book Series

Candle-Making
Coloring Papers
Nail Sculpture
Potato Printing

Translated by Paul Kuttner

88480

Contents

This is the assemblage of tools you will need for creating decorative works from ordinary nails.

Materials, Tools and Methods

When working with nails, you know that the purpose for their existence is to hold things together and you know that there are various kinds of nails. This book will deal exclusively with nails made of iron which can at long last be released from their plainness and their uniform clumsy existence, and be converted to a beautiful new appearance. Therefore the pictures in this book are not to serve so much as models to be slavishly imitated, but to provide a stimulus for new ideas and discoveries.

You can use all manner of iron nails: brads in every sort of shape, U-shaped staples, forged nails, etc., provided they are free of rust, grease and dirt.

To join nails you will have to buy some soft solder (acid core) for iron in a hardware or arts and crafts store. The commonly used multicore solder sticks only to non-ferrous (copper and brass) metals and cannot be used for your purpose here.

In fact, it is best for you to use rosin flux also because the chemical components found in the soft solder often are not sufficiently potent to remove the oxide coating residuals adhering to the nails. A bond cannot be achieved unless all oxides are removed.

For soldering, you will need a soldering iron (100-150 watts) and, if possible, a soldering torch (Ronson sells one) or the larger size butane burner which is also used for camping and outdoor cooking.

This equipment is available in many hardware stores, arts and crafts shops and larger department stores.

To bend nails you must have at least two pairs of pliers (best of all are some universal pliers used for pinching off nails); also a small vise to help bend the heavier nails would be most helpful in this hobby. (But many charming little pieces of work can be achieved by using only straight or hand-bent nails.)

Now you have to obtain a heat-resistant base. In a number of cases you can get by with a firebrick or an ordinary brick; for more complex work it is advisable to place an asbestos mat about $\frac{3}{8}$-inch-thick over the brick—or bricks, depending on the size of your project. Besides this, you can actually impale or fix the nails on the asbestos mat, arranging them prior to soldering in the structural pattern that you plan to achieve in your end product.

Step 1. Very few tools are needed—common nails, a soldering iron, acid-core solder, rosin flux, pliers and perhaps a hammer and a small vise. Here the work is done on a patio brick, but an asbestos mat can be used as well.

5

Step 2. *After the rosin flux has been applied, the nails are joined together by heating the solder with the iron and letting it flow over the joint.*

The soldering process itself is relatively simple. The cleaned parts you intend to join together are first heated with the soldering iron or torch, then dabbed with some flux. Next you intensify the heat to the fusion or melting temperature of the solder. Now the solder itself is applied by melting it with the tip of the iron until it flows on to the joint. At all times see to it that the scale is removed from the tip of the soldering iron. File the scale off and "re-tin" the copper tip by dipping it in rosin and then coating it well with solder.

Most mishaps during the soldering process can be attributed to the fact that the point of fusion, the point where the parts are to be joined, has not been heated sufficiently.

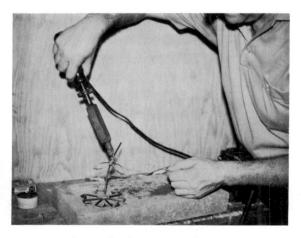

Step 3. *Here the stem has been joined to the petals. The leaves, which have been wired in place, are being soldered to the stem.*

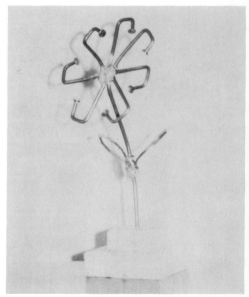

Step 4.

The finished piece is a floral sculpture made of common nails and inserted in a wooden base for display.

The butane soldering torch has an advantage over the soldering iron in that it heats the joints much faster and over a wider area and, as a consequence, manages to spread the flux of the solder to every part of the point of fusion. On the other hand, you must take care while using the torch that you do not overheat the nails, because this will cause strong oxidization, and the solder cannot then be absorbed. In such an emergency, it helps to clean the nails again and touch them up with flux.

For flat designs no special preparation or equipment is necessary to join the nails. You simply place the nails in any shape or design you want on the base support, heat the joints, preferably with the soldering torch, and let the solder flow. For such works, it is of great value to give the solder you use an aesthetic appearance of its own; therefore do not be too economical with it here.

For upright structures, work your way up directly from your brick or asbestos base: add nail to soldered nail. When you start on such a project you will soon become aware that your own two hands will not be enough to complete the assignment. You will need an assistant. Your friend's job will be to hold the nail with his pliers in such a way that you can fuse it to another nail with a soldering iron and soft solder wire. Your assistant must hold the nail absolutely still and serve you as well by handing you further equipment such as pliers. The soldering torch is not well-suited for such structural projects because it would heat up too large an area and as a consequence dissolve those spots that have already been soldered.

If you cannot get an assistant, then place part of your structural project in a pre-fixed position by hammering it into the base, forcing it into pieces of brickwork, or holding the parts together with wire which you later remove.

You will see many combinations of flat and structural projects in the illustrations of this book.

After the pieces are finished, they have to be cleaned of greasy solder residuals in a hot alkaline solution or detergent soap with a soft brush. The reason for this is that otherwise deposits of rust form on the iron soon after soldering (due to the acid in the flux). In order to guard the completed projects still further against rust, the application of an anti-rust preparation is recommended or a coating with colorless varnish, or both. These products are available in paint stores.

7

Step 1. The straight iron nail on the left will have to be bent to the final form shown on the right in order to construct the candleholder seen on page 43.

Step 3. When you have enough nails formed in this manner, arrange them in a circle on your patio brick or asbestos mat.

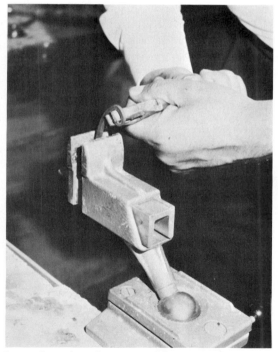

Step 2. Secure the nail in a vise and firmly bend it to the desired shape with a pair of universal pliers.

Step 4. Solder the heads of the nails together with a butane torch. Do not overheat the nails or you will have to clean them and start over again.

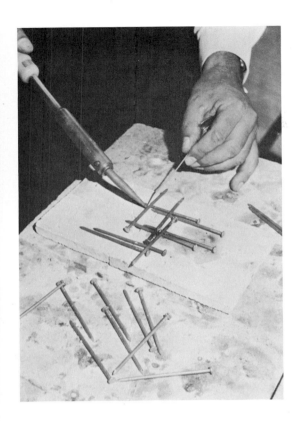

The nails in this flat construction are being joined together with a soldering iron. After heating the metal, apply the solder by melting it with the tip of the iron until if flows on to the joint.

You can also use a butane torch to heat the metal and melt the solder. The torch works faster than the soldering iron and distributes the heat over a wider area, but it requires more experience to obtain exact control of the equipment.

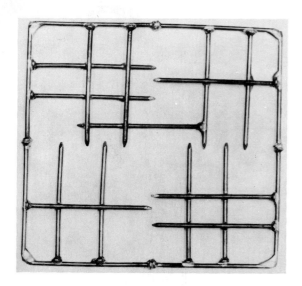

Simple, Flat-Surface
Projects with Straight Nails

Within a rectangular frame, straight nails are soldered at right angles to each other. This and the following eight projects are all flat-surface works executed with a soldering torch.

Nails soldered at varying angles form a wide range of shapes within the frame.

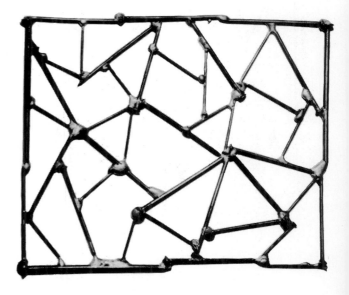

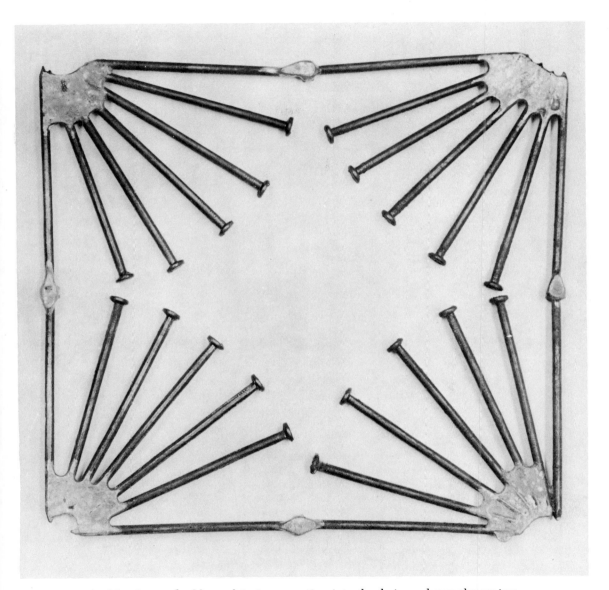

The liberal use of solder and its incorporation into the design enhance the project.

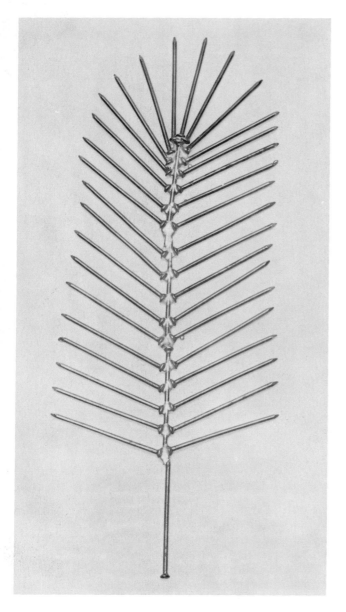

A straight row of nails provides the base for this leaf-like form. Solder the other nails to the base with their points facing outward. For a circular design (opposite page, top) solder nails together with the heads pointing outward.

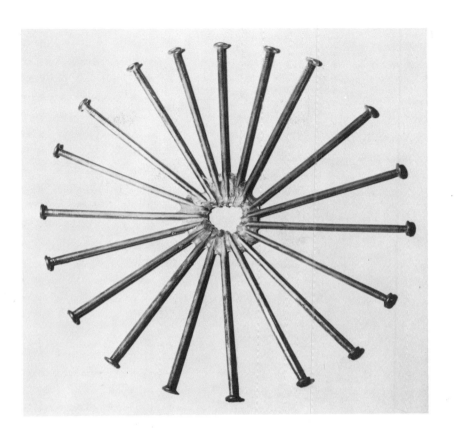

You can use the methods described in this book even for lettering.

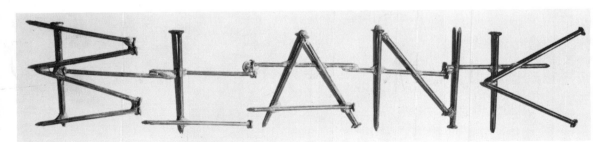

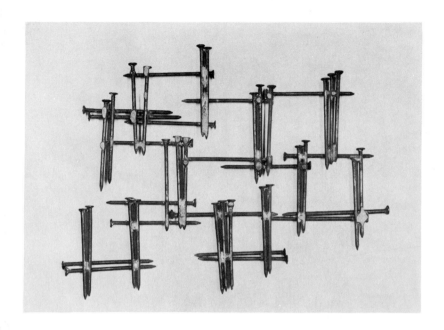

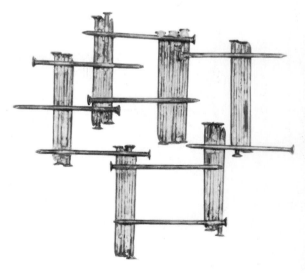

Two similar compositions achieve individu-
ality by the variation in nail placement and the
inclusion of solder into the design.

14

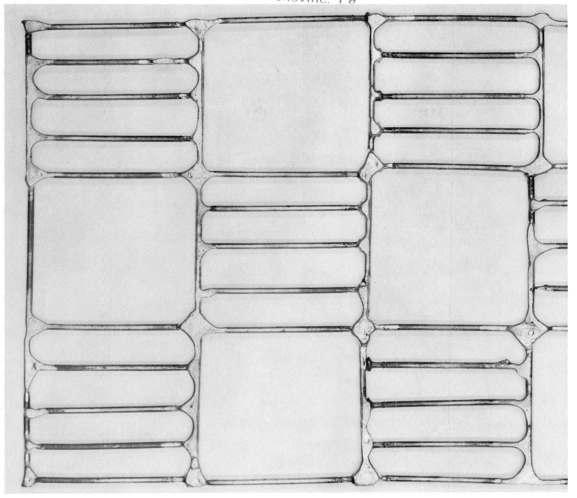

Besides joining the nails together, solder is used to hide the heads and points, leaving smooth, clean lines.

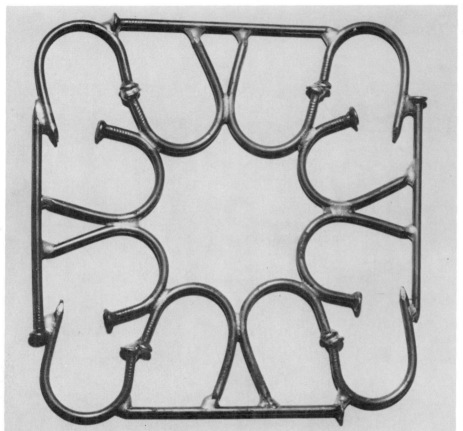

The above and the following three designs are flat-surface works made of crooked and bent nails with a soldering torch.

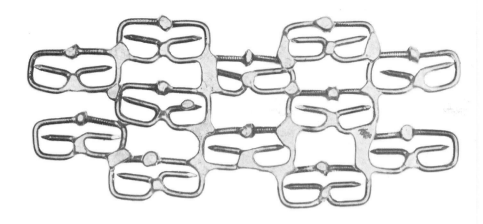

The above pattern is composed entirely of bent nails, while the one below combines bent nails with straight ones.

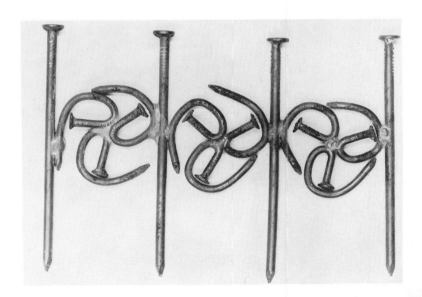

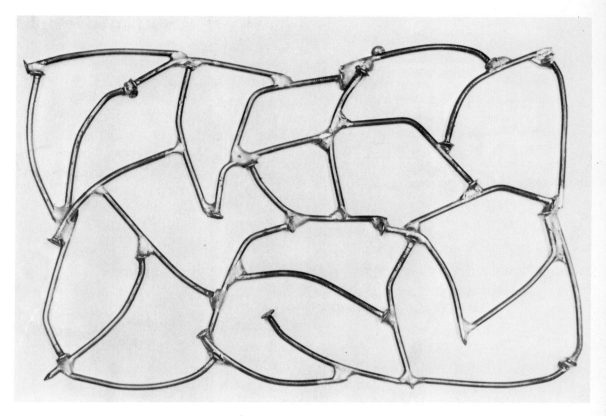

While the preceding project employed identically-bent nails, this one uses an assortment of differently shaped nails.

On this page and the next are two flat-surface works made with bent iron nails (aided by soldering torch).

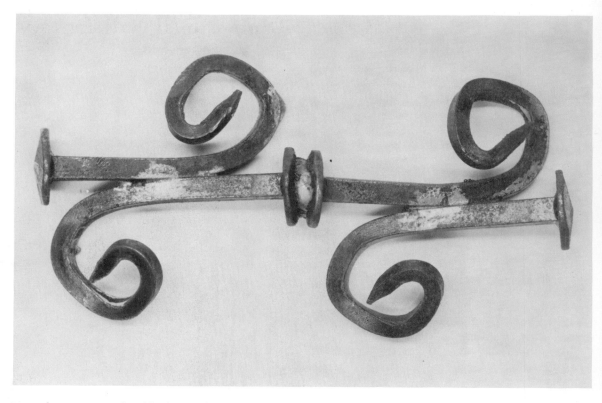

Using heavy iron nails adds a Spanish or Mexican spirit to your work.

A Three-Dimensional Nail Fantasy

A three-dimensional nail fantasy is made of wire nails (brads). Place a few nails bouquet-like into the hollow or depression of a firebrick and then fill out this space with the help of some solder and a soldering torch. Finally bend three nails head down so they can serve as the base-foundation of this "fantasy."

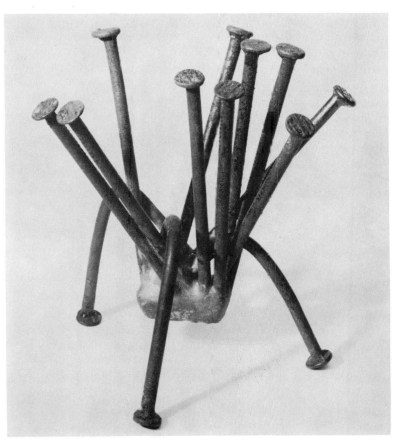

Floral Constructions

This is a three-dimensional Edelweiss. The "open blossom" and base are made by flattening U-hooked iron staples with a hammer and soldering them together with the flat-surface work technique. The "half-open blossom" and "stem" are now impaled, head-up, in the asbestos mat for the purpose of soldering. Finally the soldering iron welds the stems into the flat foundation.

The heads of these flowers are soldered in flat-work construction; the round flowers are made of bent nails of which you must first pinch off their heads. Following this, you solder the "stems" (ordinary pieces of wire) to the flower heads.

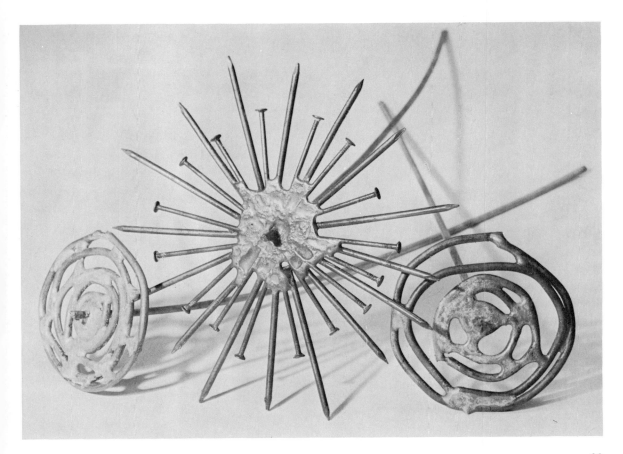

Insect and Animal Forms

Bend the nails forming the feet of this centipede. Then solder them together at their heads with the soldering iron. For this project you will need a helper to hold the nails in place.

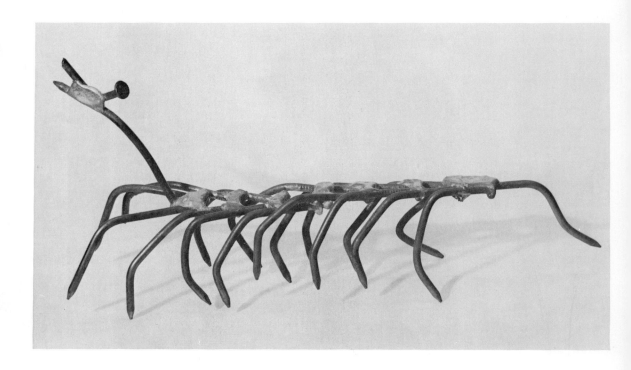

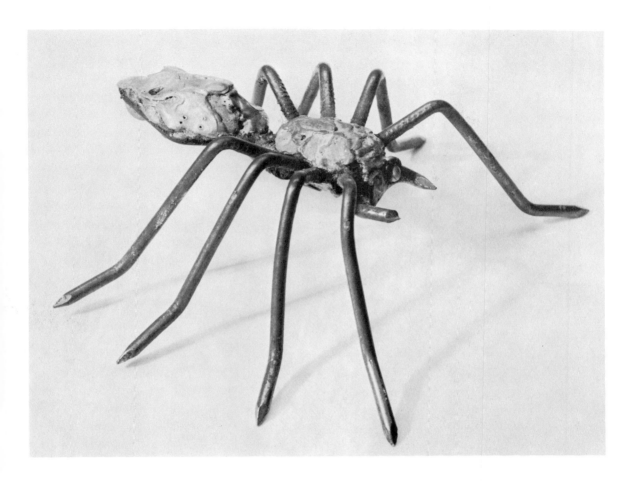

The contour of this spider body is made up of tightly coiled or twisted nails which were then soldered into one lump. As the next step, you fasten the legs to the body with the soldering iron and, finally, the body is rounded out by the soldering process.

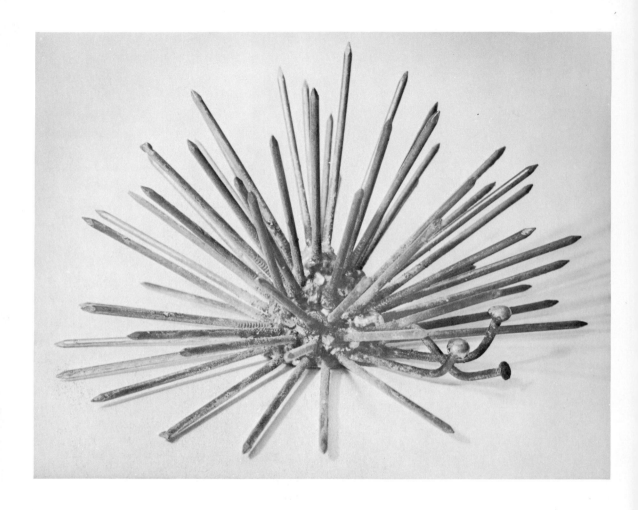

To start with, the foundation for this porcupine must be made by soldering together the heads of nails into a flattened star-like base. Next, fasten the "quills" nail by nail to the body with the iron.

When it comes to the "eyes" and the "mouth," you reverse the process and solder the point-ends of the nails to the porcupine's body.

Build up this sea urchin as you would the porcupine, starting with a star-like base, then expand to a fully rounded ball. Or simply solder two porcupines (without mouth and eyes, of course) together at their flat-base foundations.

A Simple
Candlestick

To make this candleholder, hammer a long nail firmly into your asbestos mat or brick foundation (it is this end of the nail which will serve as the candleholder later). Bend six nails at a right angle directly under their heads in such a way that they are all equally long after you have given them their new shape. Now solder them in a star-like pattern, their heads facing down, to the vertical nail. After that, you can press the whole structure of the vertical nail deeply into the asbestos mat and attach the three foundation nails to the head of the standing nail. After the three nails have been soldered, each head can be bent so that together they form an elevated structure.

An Octagonal Cage

This three-dimensional work is made of equally long nails. You build it up by basing it on an octagonal foundation, soldering nail to nail over it.

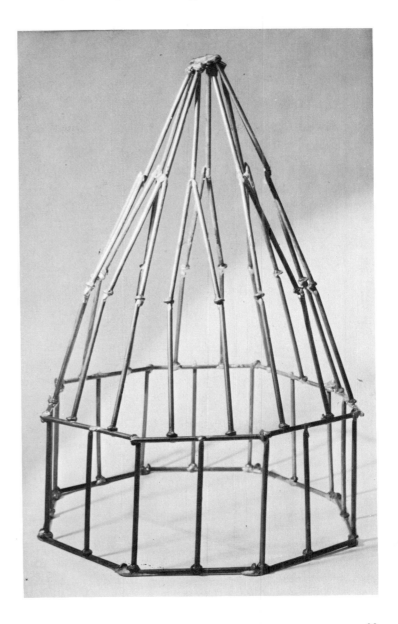

In this lantern project many nails, looking deceptively natural the way they have been bent, are fixed one to the other with a soldering iron. The nails of this lantern had been pulled out of the wood, into which they had been hammered for bending, with a pair of pincers.

Four Lantern
Projects for Candles

Use equally long nails in this flat-work construction and then solder them together in a hollow, rectangular shape with an iron. The candle is supported by a nail bent at a right angle while its head is soldered to one of the base corners of the lantern. The particular charm of these lanterns is the silhouette cast by the burning candle.

Use a round contour as the pattern for this candleholder. The nails must be of equal length and uniformly bent according to the design you have made before embarking on this project. They are fastened together with the soldering iron. The candle is impaled on a nail exactly as it was in the other projects.

For this lantern, attach one nail to another with your soldering iron to make a hollow, abstract form. The nail supporting the globular candle must be heated and bent up directly above its tip at a right angle and soldered with its head to the lantern structure.

A Decorative Sconce

This sconce consists of three flat-surface designs. A soldering torch is used for the straight and bent nails. The wedge-shaped parts at each side are fastened to the middle piece with a soldering iron.

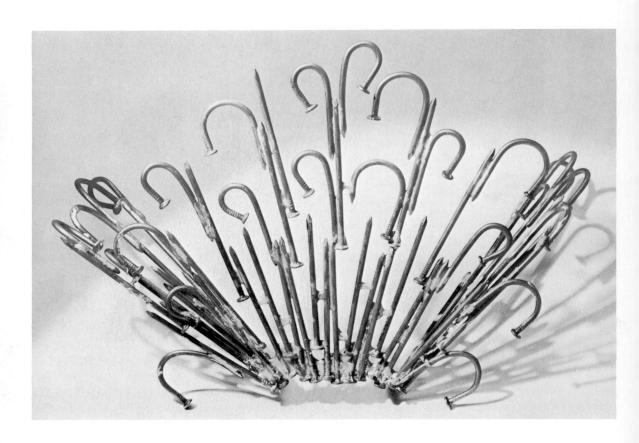

A Basket

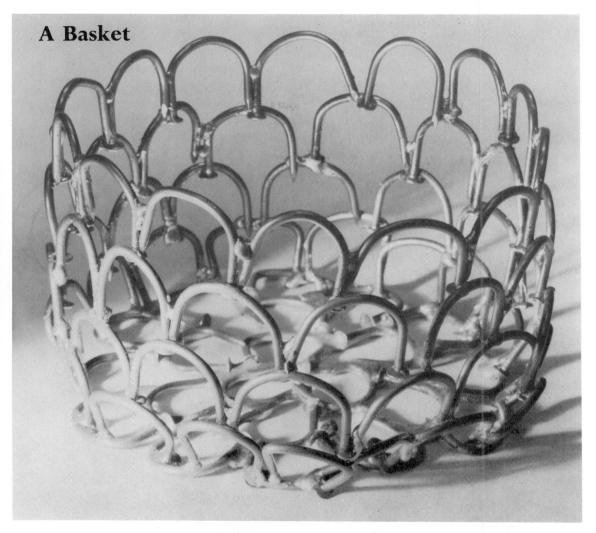

The fundamental component of this basket construction is hemispheric-ally-shaped nails. The base of the basket is a flat-surface work completed with a soldering iron and it is to this finished foundation that you weld its sides, arch by arch.

Lampshade

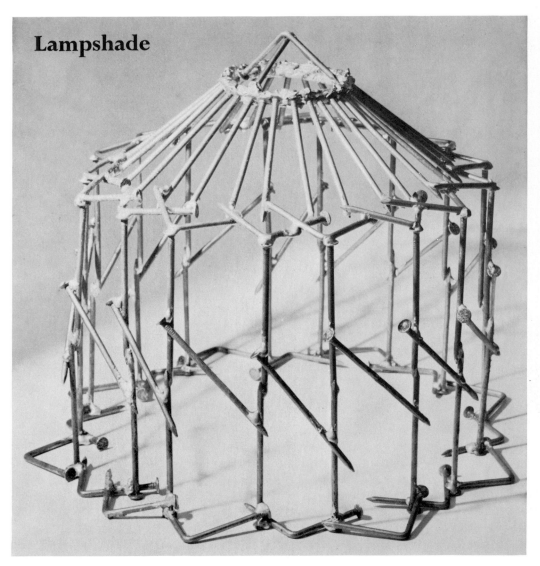

This lampshade is soldered of straight and bent nails. When it is finally placed over a burning bulb the result is a fascinating silhouette.

Abstract Construction

The basic element of this abstract work is made up of rectangularly bent nails which form an appealing structure when soldered together with an iron.

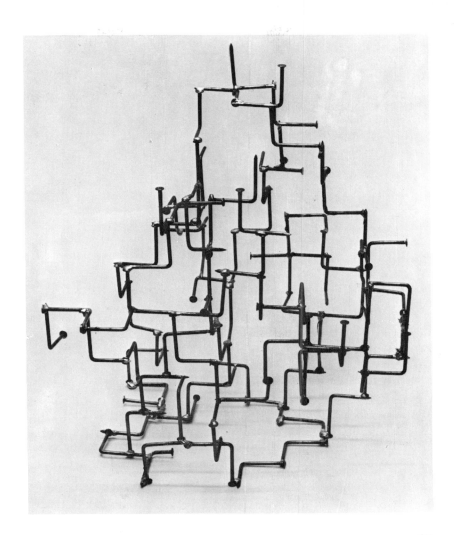

Primrose
Sculpture

The great attraction of this primrose project is that the work is completed with nails all the same size. The pistil and stem of each blossom are one and the same nail. After pressing the head of the nail into the asbestos mat so the nail stands upright, attach symmetrically bent nails to it with a soldering torch. These star-like shapes serve as petals. The nails providing the base are bent only after they have been soldered to the stem.

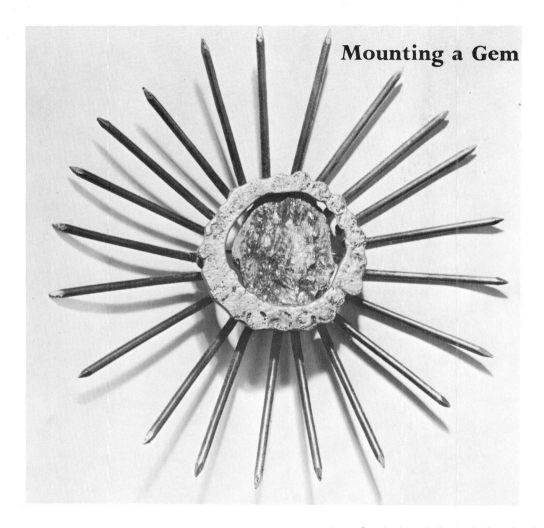

Mounting a Gem

Just as in the case of the candleholder, you bend a large number of nails directly beneath their heads at a right angle and solder them together head-down in a star-like formation with the soldering torch. This time, however, you will be making an unusual setting in which to mount a gem. Use a generous amount of flux. To prevent the nails from falling down, you can push their tips into the asbestos mat. The gem can be fastened with wire inside the soldering circle.

Ornate Wrought Iron Works

Place a heavy, iron nail head-down on your support. This nail serves as your candleholder. Since the head of the nail is slightly rounded you have to file it a bit until it is even and flat and can stand upright without wobbling. Place identically curved nails now around the center spike and solder them together with an iron. As the following picture shows this center spike can also be made into a twisted shape. Screw the iron spike head-down into a vise and make it red-hot with the soldering flame; then twist it into shape. The ornament can greatly gain in appeal.

A thick candle is the ideal accompaniment to the candleholder seen on the previous two pages.

After bending a number of nails to an identical shape with the aid of a vise and some universal pliers, place them in a circle on your mat support so that the heads touch. Heat the heads with an iron and solder them together.

Components needed for this wreath are wrought iron nails of equal size which have been given identical curvatures without heat. The bottom support must be larger in this project than in the case of the other designs. (In any case, never solder on concrete or ordinary stone. There is always the danger of injury through a sudden ricochet.) At first make an outline of the circle on the asbestos mat, sketching in the arrangement of each separate group of nails. After placing the bent nails correctly and in the right order on the mat, you can solder them one to the other where they touch. Finally solder four pinched-off nails to the crown for placement of the candles.

This sconce is a flat-surface project made of identically curved wrought iron nails. The candle is impaled on a nail bent up at a right angle while the head of this nail is soldered to the flat wall bracket.

Once again the four sides are prepared separately on a flat surface with the soldering torch and joined into one rectangular piece with the help of a soldering iron. Nevertheless, this time you may use nails of different sizes.

46

Index